A GLOSSARY OF PC TOSSERY

Andrew Lawrence

Welcome Comrades!

To begin, a humble enquiry:
Do you find yourself, like so many these days, deeply troubled by this increasingly fascistic world?
Oh, you do?
And have you noticed a worrying prevalence of anger and bigotry, where there should be compassion and understanding?
Oh, you have?
Well then, how lucky that you've stumbled upon this weighty tome.
For the times we live in are bleak indeed.

Outside your front door this toxic world is a teeming mass of sexist, racist, Islamo/homo/transphobic scum- ignorant and full of hate. Everywhere you turn, an upsurge of intolerance.

This is, of course, the legacy of capitalism. A rotten world overrun with greedy, selfish oafs, all trampling upon each other to accumulate wealth and power.
A world where we are each of us trapped in endless, vile competition with one another, in a meaningless race to scale the social and financial ladders of vulgarity.

In such a world, who is looking after the vulnerable and needy, the women, the ethnic minorities, the disabled, the gays, the ladyboys, the midgets and the enormous fat bastards who can't get off the sofa without a winch?

No-one!- These unfortunate, victimised souls are discriminated against every second, of every minute, of every hour, of every day. Their lives are an absolute living hell.

And who is it that makes their lives a living hell?

Straight, white men- that's who!

Straight, white men- society structured in their favour, handed everything on a plate in life, lording it over everyone else.

Straight, white men- who from the moment of birth, have opportunities for

improvement, education and advancement chucked at them left, right and centre.
Straight, white men- who have wealth and status automatically showered upon them, whilst everyone else in society suffers in penury.
How can we save the world from all of this obscenity and unfairness?
Why, by adopting a tyrannical attitude towards freedom of expression of course!

Anyone, anywhere, in any context, who says or does something that might be interpreted as in any way bigoted or discriminatory towards women, ethnic minorities, disabled people, the LGBTQ community- or indeed any group within society that, as Leftists, we deem to be vulnerable, must be mercilessly and publicly shamed for as long as it takes to ruin that individual's life completely. We must destroy these hateful creatures both professionally and socially. Intolerance must not be tolerated under any circumstances.

As Leftists, 'Live and let live' should be our creed, but yet at the same time, let us do everything within our power to ensure that anyone who carries a whiff of prejudice about them experiences life at its most miserable.

Let us create a wonderful culture of fear, where everyone is terrified of saying or doing the wrong thing. And when the unwashed masses are sufficiently intimidated, we will finally be able to create the Marxist utopia that this world was always destined to become.

And so, Comrades, read on then, educate yourselves as to the ways of political correctness and spread the good news to others.

A
Altruism:

A capacity for selfless kindness, indisputably present in all human beings, except for those who haven't embraced Leftism yet, who may not really even be human at all, but shape-shifting lizards from an evil planet, who have invaded Earth in order to corrupt mankind, which in its natural state is 100% Marxist in its values.

Compassion, empathy, kindness- these are words that are exclusively attributable to the Left- and anyone who isn't one of us may as well be carrying a neon sign above their head saying 'Nasty, Selfish Git'.

Steer clear of these despicable creatures. If they cross your path, give them the widest of berths- for they would probably trip you up and kick you into the road if they could.

Anti-Semitism:

A thorny term to have to negotiate so early in the book, no doubt, but that is the peril of alphabetisation for you. Let us approach the subject of anti-Semitism without fear or caution.

Undoubtedly, we can all agree that anti-Semitism constitutes anything remotely negative a non-Jewish person might have to say about any Jewish person.

Clearly, if there is a Jewish person in your life that you want to level some sort of criticism at, it cannot possibly be because they've done anything wrong. It can only be because you hate all Jewish people- and like Hitler, you would try to kill them all, if you had the chance.

It is vital that all Jewish people be able to say and do whatever they please without being subject to any kind of criticism, because as soon as you criticise one Jew, it all escalates very quickly into a Holocaust-type scenario, and that sort of thing is best avoided.

Criticise whoever you want, bad-mouth whoever you want, but not a Jewish person, because of all the horror that history has shown us. Just let them get on with doing what they want to do, because every Jew is actually a faultless paragon of virtue and must be treated as such, always.

Asylum seeker:

These poor people must be accepted into our country without question and given all the financial support they need to thrive in our society.

If an individual from a foreign land claims that they are fleeing an oppressive regime and that their life is endangered, then we must give them credence.

There are some despicable, cynical people in this world who bizarrely believe that long-suffering, oppressed individuals from the world's most dangerous places would somehow choose to lie about their situations.

There are some deluded fools who genuinely believe that many asylum seekers are actually little more than economic migrants, looking to take advantage of our uniquely generous benefits system, make money and enjoy excellent quality of life in our fine country.

Even if this were the case (which it jolly well isn't), who are we to deny them?

What makes any of us think we are somehow the only ones entitled to enjoy life in this country, just because we are lucky enough to hold citizenship here through accident of birth, and have paid taxes here all our lives?

Yes, yes, undoubtedly many white British people are given a poor deal by the state. They are provided with a poor education and left to languish in council bedsits. They are crack-addled to a degree where they haven't noticed that the establishment cares more about newly arrived immigrants than it does about them. Blah, blah, blah. So what? In the grand scheme of things, that's not important is it? Let's not be churlish. Let's remember, always, that we are first and foremost citizens of the world.

Tear down the walls, scrub out all the borders, let us move freely amongst each other.

Let people from the world's harshest places come and enjoy the thriving democracy that our fathers and grandfathers built for us through great personal sacrifice, and let these new arrivals freely transform our home with their own values and customs so that it becomes just like their own home, which they chose to abandon. Who could object to that, other than a hideous racist?

Austerity:

The despicable Tories, a noxious blend of psychopaths, toffs, chancers and thieves, having somehow, through cloak and dagger means, seized a strong electoral mandate to govern the country, have proceeded to bloody well use that mandate to set about dismantling the welfare state- vigorously attacking the benefits system in an effort to kill off all the poor, the needy and the disabled people. The unpardonable, murderous pigs.

Many people who can't work because they've got a gammy leg, or they get tired a lot, or they feel sad all the time, are being forced to live off state hand-outs of less than a pound a week. They have no choice but to eat pigeon poop scrapped off park benches, and household pets. They sleep on a pile of used toilet paper, because the Tories hate them and want them all to die. It is imperative that we get rid of these Tory scumbags at the next election- by controlled explosion if necessary.

B

BBC:

A wonderful sanctuary for the Jewish community of North London, paedophiles and gay people. A place where they can be showered with millions of pounds of licence fee cash, without needing to have any discernible talent, just a rigid smile and indestructible levels of self-esteem.

The BBC's role in society is to pump Marxist propaganda into everybody's home night after night, until everyone is certain in the knowledge that there is only one truth in this world- that progress and ultimate happiness for all of us lies in the unrelenting pursuit of 'Equality' and 'Diversity'- which, of course, are brilliant new words that have been made up to describe the 'Positive Discrimination' that most people all stupidly rejected when the BBC tried to foist it on them in the eighties. All bloody credit to the Beeb for having a second crack at it. If at first you don't succeed, try, try again, until everyone's satisfactorily indoctrinated.

Bigot:

This word broadly encompasses anybody who contradicts any of our beliefs, or thinks it's OK to make hilarious 'jokes' about what we consider to be protected, vulnerable groups within society. It isn't OK. It is sick and it is vile to make such jokes and any peddlers of such ordure should be rooted out, shamed, punished and ostracised in the severest manner. Let there be no mercy for them, for their crime in a heinous one, the crime of independent thought.

Black people:

Why are you categorising? They are not 'Black' people. They are just people. Ordinary people just trying to live their lives, just trying to get through each day. Just like you and me, trying to cope with everything the world throws at them.

We are all the same. We are all one. One love. One life. One world. They are not 'Black' people, they are HUMAN BEINGS. They just want to be treated like everybody else, and once they are, maybe they'll stop stealing.

Body shaming:

Human beings come in many shapes and sizes, and some of them are truly disgusting. But when will people understand that it's OK to be disgusting?

Do people spontaneously throw up their lunch every time you take your t-shirt off? Oh, they do? Well that's OK my friend. You have nothing to be ashamed of. There's nothing wrong with you. You just happen to look like shit, that's all, and that's fine, it's alright, it's no big deal.

And you could probably change the way you look through regular exercise, but why should you put yourself through such sweaty unpleasantness just to accommodate the shallow standards of physical beauty deemed acceptable by a broken, sick society? Let it all hang out mate.

Brexit:

The clearest proof that anyone could ever need that people in general are far too ignorant to deserve democracy.
Why would anyone, in the name of all that is sacred, actually choose to leave such a flawless, efficient, impeccably run institution like the EU?
What will any of us do without its endless flowing red tape?
How will we live without it's all-pervading petty bureaucracy?
Why wouldn't we all want every resident of every EU member state to have unrestricted access to the UK and its benefits system?
There can be no doubt- people who voted for Brexit did so because they are

racist imbeciles- all seventeen and a half million of them.

It is imperative that we work towards a society where these people will not have the right to vote anymore- as they have proved themselves incapable of using their vote responsibly, fascist scumbags.

Brown people:

Just like black people, but a bit paler. Similar to white people, but darker. Hairier than oriental people, smellier than gingers. Try not to get stuck behind them at airport security.

C

Capitalism:

The sole source of all evil in this world. The font from which all misery springs. A hierarchical shit-pile of greed and bigotry. That's all I will say about that. I'm so angry about Capitalism, I could spit out my frappucino and scream, even now as I sit here behind my Apple MacBook in this busy Starbucks. Fuck you Starbucks. Fuck you Apple. You represent everything I hate, but please sell me some more of your over-priced crap, so that I can walk around with the same stuff everyone else has got and feel like I fit in.

I hate Capitalism and I hate myself because I can't stop consuming. And I know that only a pure and disciplined devotion to Marxism can save me from a vile, wasted life of shopping. I will unburden myself of material concerns, and so must we all, for if we don't, eventually we will all be buried under the collective weight of our plastic landfill, willing accomplices in our own extinction.

Censorship:

I wrote at length under this heading, but upon consideration, decided not to publish what I'd written, because I suspect it may have upset some of you- and I care deeply about your well-being, as I am person of exceptional empathy. Instead of reading whatever traumatic thing it is that I had to say, close your eyes and think of a unicorn tap-dancing across a rainbow, and as that image fades in your imagination, don't be afraid to have a little cry- we all need one from time to time.

Always remember you are beautiful, you are special and you are loved, even though there is no evidence of any of those things.

Block out the bad thoughts, block out the bad words, block out the nasty truth and believe whatever makes you happy.

Charity:

Thank God (A non-specific God, who probably doesn't exist anyway actually, because look at the state of the world) Thank God, that when the governments and the powerful people of this planet neglect their duty to their fellow human beings, there are selfless, benevolent individuals who organise into collectives and fundraise tirelessly so that they can swoop to the rescue of all those poor, forgotten victims the Establishment does not care about.

The governments and the rich and influential people of this world have no care for their fellow human beings.

They feel no empathy for those in need. They'd sooner tread them into the ground than spare them the merest scrap of kindness.

But from the shadows of society's ills emerge the true heroes of humanity. Those who put others before themselves. People who run charities. Tireless humanitarians. Many asking nothing in return for their efforts other than a six figure salary drawn from the charitable donations that they have coerced from people.

Charity workers are so eager to help humankind and make the world a better place that they will accost you in the street to ask for your money, or phone you in your own home late in the evening, or post leaflets through your letterbox emblazoned with harrowing images of children suffering, or spend hundreds of thousands of pounds of people's charitable donations to put an advert for their charity on television, with some homeless guy in a sleeping bag crying and hugging his sad, emaciated dog, with a voiceover by some famous, worthy actor who's agreed to help out by offering a discount of ten per cent on his usual performance fee.

Yes, yes, people who work for charities occasionally take advantage of their position of trust by lining their own pockets, or lying to their donors, or cooking their books, or only turning up at work half the time, but they are undeniably souls of pure intention. They desperately want to help the poor and the needy and just anyone who can convincingly manage to claim some sort of victimhood.

Why shouldn't people who work for charities get paid absolutely top dollar? They're helping the desperate and deprived of this world by collecting a load of money on their behalf and then passing a miniscule portion of it on to them.

We must always remember and appreciate that if it were not for charities, then needy people would have nothing- so they should shut up with their whining and just be grateful for what little they do get, or otherwise hurry up and die.

Colonialism:

Never let us forgot, that evil white people travelled the earth for generations stealing everything they could from black and brown people. Stealing their culture, their land, their natural resources, and then enslaving them. This happened from the 1600's onwards, and before this period, all history is irrelevant.

In order to heal, as one species, sharing one planet, evil white people must acknowledge and accept responsibility for the crimes of their ancestors, and start to pay back the massive debt that they owe to brown and black people.

The privileged, luxury, easy lives that all white people enjoy, are built upon the sorrow, indignity, oppression and back-breaking work of brown and black people- who are all pure in soul, and free of guilt.

Since the beginning of time, whilst white people have consistently indulged in nothing but savagery and evil, all people of colour have lived virtuous lives.

Since the beginning of time, people of colour have walked the planet as angels, tending the earth and protecting all forms of life, living in peace and harmony and goodness- only to be brutally taken advantage of by white devils.

The only sort of good earth, the only truly beautiful world to live in, is one without pasty, white evil spirits who were, in the beginning, probably just summoned here by Satan himself. Scientifically speaking, we can say that all evidence suggests that whiteness is the outward sign of a lack of evolutionary progress. May they all burn in the hot sun. May they burn to ashes that float across the earth and eventually all just land together in a massive bin, a bin full of racist dust.

Comrade:

One of us. A bone fide, signed-up, extra-sensitive, tree-hugging, refugee-loving, eco-friendly, feminist, vegan, bi-sexual, privileged-white-male-hating, special snowflake, social justice warrior, paid-up member of the hammer and sickle brigade. The future of this country.

We are on a higher plane of intellectual thought and together we can cleanse the world of prejudice. If only the ignorant masses would listen to us and do what we tell them, for we are the chosen ones.

Cultural Appropriation:

Look, dreadlocks are for black people, rap music is for black people, kimonos are for Japanese people, headdresses are for indigenous Americans, potatoes are for Irish people, comedy is for Jewish people, bagpipes are for Scottish people, curry is for Indian people, Christmas is for Christians, suicide bombing is for Muslims. And if you're not one of those groups of people, don't start using any of their stuff. They invented those things for themselves, not for you, arsehole. Find your own identity and stop trying to steal other peoples.

Haven't you stolen enough from vulnerable minority groups already, white devil?
Haven't you used colonialism as an excuse to travel the world, taking advantage of innocent people's benevolence and kindness to thieve them of their culture and all their natural resources?
Yes, you have, and I have too.
For we are white- it is the colour of shame.
Are you white?- Then why aren't you busy hating yourself.

D
Democracy:

The very idea that people should have the power to choose representatives to govern the land that they all share together is palpable madness.

How have we got ourselves into this terrible mess of ordinary people having a vote and being able to elect politicians to run the country?

Who thought it was a good idea to give every single, dribbling, mono-browed Neanderthal a say in how the world is shaped around them?

It is the most despicable tragedy of our times, people having the power and freedom to govern their own lives.

As all Comrades know, the general populace is comprised of imbeciles. Worthless, inbred filth who can't be trusted to put the right bin out for collection, let alone pick the right government.

Much better that a small circle of wealthy, metropolitan North London, public school, Oxbridge über-Comrades should decide who governs the country- if not the entire world. Better still, they could run the country themselves on a job-share basis from a vegan café in Islington.

It's time that everyone learned to accept that wealthy North London Leftists are not at all smug and condescending, but that they genuinely are more intelligent than everyone else, they truly are right about everything, and they certainly know, one hundred percent, what's best for us all.

Demonstration:

Jolly well making extra-special nuisances of ourselves by congregating with home-made banners bearing words of rare wisdom and moral integrity.

Filling the streets with noble chants of righteous conviction, in an effort to disrupt people's day in major city centres, in protest at the evil, democratically elected cretins that run this country- who won't give us what we've asked for, what we want, and what we know is right, just because the vast majority of utter dribbling plebs in this sorry excuse of a nation don't agree with us.

We're so bloody middle-class it hurts, and we want everyone to know about it.

And we may or may not stop half way through our demonstration for an overpriced fair trade mochaccino and a salt-beef bagel as we march through the organic farmers' market- and why the bloody hell shouldn't we? We're so socially aware and morally engaged we sodding well deserve the odd treat whilst we're smashing the system to smithereens.

Disablism:

For heaven's sake, If we're not going to pass a law to obligate the termination of all faulty babies during pregnancy, then the very least we can do after they're born is pretend that they're normal and that they can do all the things that everyone else can.

There's no sense, or decency, in being nasty. They've got enough to deal with, the special people- what with the dribbling and the incontinence and the clunky chairs they've got to wheel round in.

Just bloody well treat them with respect, poor things.

And thank God, that glorious, wonderful, socially-aware Channel 4 now has blanket, twenty-four-hour coverage of the Paralympic games, because it is vital that we all watch non-standard people doing sport and convince ourselves that we're interested in it and impressed by it all. Three cheers for all the elite dribblers falling over themselves! Hip-hip hooray!

Discrimination:

Always remember- we must never, ever discriminate against people based on their gender or ethnicity. Unless their gender is male, and their ethnicity is white.

If helping the progress of poor, oppressed women and people of colour in society means scuppering the advancement of white men- who have had it far too easy for far too long- then that is the path we must follow.

Merit does not come into it. The world is so racist and sexist, we simply cannot give people opportunities based on their abilities anymore.

We must worship at the altar of positive discrimination- push ethnic minority and female candidates into well-paid positions of power and influence in society, regardless of whether they have the requisite experience, qualifications, natural ability or intelligence for the position in question. This is how we will instigate true social change.

The only way to smash inequality and create a fair society, is to make sure there is not a level playing field.

Diversity:

A bloody marvellous compulsory employment strategy for all UK businesses.

It is quite rightly unacceptable these days for the staff of any organisation not to look like a human rainbow. Businesses must employ people of all different hues and nationalities and backgrounds and genders and religions and sexual preferences, regardless of suitability, or experience, or qualifications for the job they are being employed to do. This is clearly a rational approach to running any efficient organisation- and anyone who says otherwise is a fascist.

In any work place these days, when it comes to employees, the important thing is not competence, but variety. To rectify the patriarchal crimes of the past, it is important that businesses employ no more than one straight, white, university educated male- and ideally that guy should be employed to empty the bins.

E

Empowerment:

Everyone knows there are oppressed, vulnerable groups in society that need special treatment and a leg-up in the world.

It is very important that, if we perceive certain people to be victims of latent social prejudice, they should be given advantages in life that they don't necessarily deserve in a literal sense.

It is only with the kind of sociological perspective that deeply intelligent people have, that merit can truly be judged anyway.

It is only by giving some individuals greater opportunities than others in society, based on vague and dubious criteria of imagined victimhood, that we can create a fair and just world for all.

Entitlement:

It is an absolute disgrace that white guys from decent homes who have worked hard all their lives- from getting good grades at school, to being a diligent employee, turning up at work on time every day and giving the absolute best of themselves- should expect to be given employment opportunities just because they're the best candidate for a job, ahead of a black, disabled lesbian who's just got out of prison.

Let's be clear about this, white guys don't deserve a damn thing. But they all imagine that they deserve everything laid on a plate for them. They automatically assume they are better than everybody else. This prejudiced, toxic mindset is ingrained in our culture. As Leftists, we call this psychological ailment 'Entitlement'- and because we have given it a definite name, we can say with absolute certainty, that it is a real thing that genuinely exists.

Equality:

We are all of us the same in our intellectual and physical abilities at birth and it is only our environment, upbringing and educational opportunities that make some of us seem better than others at stuff. That is a proven fact.

Consequently, in a just and fair world, if some individuals have had more opportunities earlier in their development than others, it is imperative that they be discriminated against later on in life.
It is vital that we harmonise on who the vulnerable groups in society are, and then make sure that they receive

advantages over and above people who are from more privileged groups within society.

Yes, yes, the idea of people being either 'vulnerable' or 'privileged' is entirely subjective, and is in no way truly verifiable, but that's not important. What is important is that, in all spheres of life, from now on, merit must not be taken into account.
Meritocracy is just a form of discrimination against people who aren't very good at stuff.

European Union:

Probably the greatest institution on earth.

For decades the EU brought the people of the UK nothing but wealth, happiness, and quality of life.

It bound us together in peace and harmony with our closest neighbours for our mutual benefit.

Together we were stronger. Together we learned to thrive and prosper.

Truly it represented the best of humanity.

Our security and safety were assured, united with our European brothers and sisters.

And then the ignorant masses of Britain, upon being foolishly granted a referendum, chose to abandon this great and beautiful, powerful edifice of human accord. Arseholes.
'It's unelected!' they said.
'It's undemocratic!' they said.
'It's exercising a degree of control over the nation that the British people never sanctioned!' they said.
'It is mired in endless red tape. It's just a gravy train for faceless bureaucrats. It acts almost solely in the best interests of its pre-eminent members- Germany and France. It's corrupt. It's biased. It's left our borders open to all and sundry!' they said.
And yes, all of those things were true.

In many ways the UK was getting screwed over by EU membership- but was it really any worse than what we face now? Uncertainty? Isolation? Economic Armageddon?
Doomed! We're all doomed. Brexit has ruined us all. We're going to hell in a hand basket. It's over. It's all over. We're ruined. We're finished.
Any day now. Seriously. The apocalypse is coming. Brexit has brought us the apocalypse.
No it's not here yet. But it's coming. When? Difficult to say.
But when it does come, every Brexit-voting bastard is going to hang their head in shame, disgusting bigots.

F

Fatism:

The abhorrent discrimination that water-retentive people face on an almost hourly basis is truly a sad indictment of our broken, fascistic society.

When did it ever enter into the collective consciousness that there was something wrong, or amusing, or bad about having a fuller figure?

Just because people eat too much and don't get enough exercise, why should they then be judged for being overweight?

Chubbychops, jellybelly big-butt, plate licker, wobbletard, sandwich smuggler, buffet botherer- these are some of the horrible names that I've just come up with that could be used to body shame fat people.

It is an absolute disgrace what they're subjected to, the fat people.

They are human beings like the rest of us.

They need compassion, understanding and friendship.

Invite them into your home, and let them know they're beautiful just the way they are. And if you want to put a lock on your fridge first, that is your prerogative as the home owner.

Talk to them, let them know they've got nothing to be ashamed of, and then make them jog around your garden until they collapse. Jog along-side them with a doughnut on the end of stick if necessary.

Do whatever it takes, just get those porkers moving before they turn diabetic. But for God's sake, stop judging them.

Feminism:

Urgh, where to start really. What an awful world it is, if you're a woman.

I suppose firstly let it be said, once and for all, that women absolutely don't need men for anything.

Yes, most women who are capable of getting a man will happily take one on board, but women who can't manage to get a man definitely don't need men at all.

Women can be perfectly happy without a man.

There are plenty of things women can do without men. Like knitting and cat breeding and crying and jam making and witchcraft.

Second of all, let it be said, that motherhood is an option, not an imperative. There are many, many happy women who have never had children, who have focused on their careers, travelled the world and can now enjoy the trappings of their success- a beautiful home, a beautiful, opulent, empty, silent home- and lots of money, mounds of cash, and best of all, no-one hanging around expecting a share of it.

Thirdly, let it be said, that all women are beautiful. Big, small, tall, fat, hairy, smelly, cross-eyed, toothless, bald. Women come in all shapes and sizes, and they are all beautiful. Not necessarily visually beautiful, but on the inside somewhere, where it really matters. And some women are not visually beautiful and are rotten on the inside as well, but they're very tidy or something else useful.

The point is, all women are precious and valuable and special and deserve to be loved. Even the ones that don't wash under their armpits, even the ones that put kittens in bins. Men, however are bastards. All men are bastards.
And the biggest bastards are the men who agree with you when you tell them that all men are bastards, because they think it'll shut you up for ten minutes. But it won't, because we're on to their tricks, the bastards.
We know full well there are no exceptions, all men are bastards. And rapists. All men are potential rapists.

Even when they're not raping you, you can bloody well guarantee that they're thinking about it. Bastards.

G

Gender fluid:

If somebody happens to drop this term into a sentence, the best thing to do is just to nod and look fascinated and concerned.

I have no more of a clue what it means than the next person, but if you can convincingly claim the label for yourself, then people will almost certainly think you're really unique and special.

There's truly nothing better than adopting a fancy label that baffles people, if you want to feel important in a world that otherwise quite rightly couldn't give a fuck about you.

H

Hate speech:

Hate speech is a marvellous catch-all term that covers any spoken or written expression that progressive people like us don't agree with.

The worst kind of hate speech can come across as amusing, or even sensible and intelligent.

Thankfully, to engage in anything deemed hate speech in the eyes of the law is now a gross act of criminality. At last!

Hate speech, now gloriously enshrined in UK law, has become a wonderful tool for shutting down debate, and generally curtailing the expression of ideas that might encourage individuals to stray from the righteous path of Leftism.

There are so many people in the world who are full of hate, and you cannot help but despise them. Why don't people understand that words can hurt?
When did talking about stuff we don't like, and people who annoy us, ever help us progress as a species?
Far better to bottle all our negative feelings up inside, until the strain of them becomes too much to bare and they end up manifesting themselves in the form of physical violence.

Hate crime:

This encompasses pretty much any negative action of any kind undertaken by any straight, white male against anyone who is not a straight, white male- because, as we all know, anyone who is not a straight, white male is a victim of patriarchal oppression. Undeniably, patriarchal oppression has devastated their lives, and so they deserve kindness, and anything directed towards them which is not verifiably kindness, is an act of criminality.

Eventually this diabolical crime of hatred will surely be punishable by law with the same severity as murder, for that is progress.

Anything can be motivated by hate- Leaving toenail clippings on the bathroom floor, farting in a lift, eating a burger on a crowded train, pissing in an alley way, walking really slowly across a zebra crossing when there are motorists waiting.
All these things could be motivated by hatred- if you choose to assume they are.
All these actions could be motivated by racial hatred, sexist hatred, homophobic hatred- if you choose to believe that's the case.

That's the beauty of hate crime, it's so open to interpretation, it could be used to describe virtually any action- all you have to do is wait until someone you don't like does something you object to, then make unprovable assumptions about their motives, and wave them bye-bye as the police bundle them into the back of a van.

Why not just accuse someone you don't like of a hate crime today? Especially if they're a bloody Tory or something! Just make a hate crime up! Anyone can do it!
Do you know someone who isn't a Leftist?
Then try to get them banged up for hate crime, it's brilliant fun!
And potentially something we could use to destroy the capitalist system for good- Just label anyone who doesn't agree with you a 'hate criminal', see them all locked up, and with all those scumbags taken care of, sit back and

rejoice as a Marxist utopia sprouts up all around you. How awesome would that be? I know, right!

Homophobia:

Say it loud, say it proud- THERE IS NOTHING WRONG WITH MEN SHUNTING THEIR PENISES INTO EACH OTHER'S ANUS HOLES WHERE POO COMES OUT OF, whether that be in the privacy of their own home, or in a bush in a public park, or in a nightclub toilet, or in the buggy aisle of Mothercare.

Furthermore, we must remember that all lesbians have a right to be miserable, sour-faced, man-hating binslugs- there's nothing wrong with that, and they aren't infringing on anybody else's wellbeing, apart from all the people who regularly come into contact with them on a day to day basis.

Furthermore, it is important that we stamp out this idea that you can only contract the HIV virus from gay sex. This idea comes from utter ignorance. It cannot be stated enough- Anyone, anywhere, can get HIV (but it is mostly gay blokes and Africans).

Human rights:

Never forget you have the right to be who you want to be and do what you want to do- even if what you're being is an arsehole and what you're doing is annoying people.

As long as it falls within the boundaries of the law, be as much of a tosser as you damn well please, for we live in a tolerant society, so you'll almost certainly get away with a fairly extreme level of dickishness before anyone picks you up on it.

Live and let live. Tolerance and respect are the cornerstones of our Liberal society. We don't all have the same values, but we all have it within us to understand and empathise with those who are different to us- or hold different views to us. All views are valid and deserve respect, as long as they are Leftist views.

People with views that do not accord with the tenets of Marxism should naturally be destroyed at all costs. Silence them by any means necessary, for only humans deserve human rights, and non-Leftists are not human, they're scum.

Humour:

All jokes must be thoroughly policed and if found to be at the expense of any vulnerable, protected minority group in society, the teller of the joke must be made an example of, punished in the severest possible terms to make sure nobody ever tries to speak such life-destroying, civilisation-threatening evil ever again.

Whether the joke was funny or not, is irrelevant.

Whether people laughed at the joke or not, is irrelevant.

If the joke, upon examination, is found to have the potential to hurt someone's feelings, it must be censored entirely, eradicated from every public forum, and the teller of the joke must be mercilessly demonised, professionally discredited and cast out in disgrace from his/her/their social group, and be forced to spend the rest of their days alone in a state of silent, sorrowful reflection. Plainly it is only with this level of ruthlessness that we can come to create a kinder society.

Immigration:

Anyone who suggests that there should be a cap on immigration, or that we should have better border controls, is straightforwardly a hideous racist.
It is ludicrous to suggest that a small island like the UK can't accommodate an infinite number of people.

What does it matter if all public services are massively under strain, there's a huge housing crisis and the transport system is completely in the toilet because of the sheer volume of people who have piled into this country in recent years?

We can build more houses, and hospitals, and schools, and roads, and bigger trains, and we can accommodate everybody, there's room for everybody, and they can all bring their unicorns with them as well.

Yes, yes it will take decades to implement these massive structural changes, during which time the pressure on public services and housing will escalate to a point where it spills over into severe civil disorder.
People punching each other to death over the last can of beans in Asda. People sleeping in wheelie bins. Hospitals erecting a canopy over the car

parking area, scattering a few sleeping bags around and declaring it an intensive care unit.

There's room for everybody, until there isn't, until the room runs out, and we all start to spill over a cliff into the sea, which wouldn't be a bad thing either, because who doesn't like swimming?

Inclusivity:

Everybody should be allowed to do whatever they want with whoever they want, regardless of suitability, practicality, qualifications, experience, social skills, personal hygiene and logistical concerns. And none of us should have the right to stand in their way.

Inclusivity means welcoming all types of people into professional and social environments who might otherwise be excluded and marginalised.

Look around your work space.

Are there any differently-abled people wheeling around being useful?

Look around your home, are there any tribal Namibians enjoying your hospitality ?
No? Then ask yourself why not.
Is it because you're prejudiced?
Why are there just a bunch of white people in your house? Why does everyone in your office have all their own limbs? Let's embrace the entire spectrum of humanity- white, black, gay, straight, midgets, disabled, shape-shifters, minotaurs, werewolves, crack peddlers, people smugglers, cannibals and mass-murders. Let's start mixing things up and really rubbing shoulders with each other.
As human beings, we always have enough in common to overcome our differences.

Find some common ground with an animal abuser today.
Share your work space with them, make them a coffee, buy them a muffin, hold their hand, stroke their hair.
One love. Let's look after each other. Let's look after everybody, even the weird bastards.

Indoctrinated:

Anyone who doesn't share our beliefs has clearly been brainwashed by Rupert Murdoch's evil media empire.

It is difficult to know whether these drooling, mind-crippled victims can break free of the propaganda which has poisoned their thought processes and be re-educated.

The only possible things that might work are electro-shock therapy, water-boarding or teeth extraction. We must find the goodness in our hearts to try these methods at least, we cannot simply leave these sick souls alone with their heads full of diabolical ideas that are so palpably wrong, and that successive governments have collaborated with the media over many years to hoodwink the masses into believing.

Isis:

These naughty buggers have unquestionably committed a lot of terrorist atrocities, leading to the tragic death of huge numbers of innocent people.

But let's not focus too much on feeling sorry for the dead people and their families, let's channel all our energies into regularly repeating this most sacred of proclamations-

'TERRORIST ATTACKS COMMITTED BY ISIS, HAVE ABSOLUTELY NOTHING TO DO WITH ISLAM.'

That's right! Let us at all times be vigilant in our awareness that terrorist attacks carried out across Europe by Muslim individuals associated with

Islamist groups, in the name of Allah, have absolutely nothing to do with Islam- and anyone that so much as hints at an association between Islam and terrorism is a bigot and a racist, even though Islam is not a race, it's a religion. Criticising Muslims is categorically racist, because they're all brown, except for the ones that aren't.

Islamophobia:

It is deeply wrong to be scared of Muslim people, just because certain Muslim people all across the world are committing terrorist atrocities, killing innocent citizens with abandon, in the name of Allah.
These terrorists, although Muslim, have absolutely nothing to do with Islam.

It is extremely ignorant to lump ordinary Muslims in with the extremist ones who are shooting random civilians, or blowing them up, or crashing lorries into pedestrian thoroughfares and killing loads of people and themselves, all in one go.

It is also wrong to associate ordinary Muslims with the Muslim men who, in several northern towns, groomed and sexually abused hundreds of children, whilst the police and councils turned a blind eye for fear of being accused of being racist.

You can't lump all Muslims in together. There are bad Muslims and there are good Muslims.
Yes, yes, it is difficult to tell the difference between the two when they're covered in a burka and you can't see their actual faces.
And yes, it's very difficult to give someone the benefit of the doubt, when it could result in you getting blown up or having your children fiddled with.

But nonetheless we should all make an active effort to be lovely to Muslim people. We should be visiting mosques, celebrating Eid, and generally embracing Islam.

And in fact, would it hurt any of us to actually convert to Islam? No it wouldn't. We should all convert to Islam.

J

Jingoism:

A vile form of nationalistic thought which advocates the use of threat and violence to achieve one's political aims. There is never any excuse for violence, and don't be afraid to challenge anyone who believes that there is. Yes, they will probably come at you with their fists eventually- but getting hit in the face is a small price to pay in the name of pacifism.

There can be no happiness upon this earth without peace.

To achieve peace, we need to eradicate all the violent people from this earth, and if that means rounding them all up in a big cage and just letting them batter each other to death, then so be it.

One should always seek to achieve one's political aims through communication, debate, compromise, respect, bribery, blackmail and sexual favours.
And if this peaceful brand of diplomacy fails, you have to accept that the world is not willing to come around to your way of thinking.
You have to accept that your arguments have failed, and that the future will not be the future that you had hoped for.

Your immediate instinct when that happens will be to go around and kick seven bells out of everybody- and yes that would make you feel better momentarily, but don't do it, because it's against your principles.

Punch yourself, punch a wall, but never punch other people, because it is not their fault that they're too ignorant to understand the truth of Marxism.

Surely with time and patience, the light of Marxism will dawn upon humanity in its full glory. Have faith, the day will come.

L

Lentils:

Nectar of the Gods. If anybody dare say to you that human beings can't survive without meat, then shake a bag of lentils at them.

Lentils! Packed with protein! Fruit of the earth! No suffering. No killing. Just nourishment. Don't think about the taste, just swallow them quickly and imagine that somewhere out there, there is a veal calf smiling at you, swishing its tale in gratitude for leaving it the fuck alone.

M

Marxism:

The only way forward. The truth. The cause. The recipe for human happiness. Yes, it hasn't really worked out that great in the past.

Some would say that the most notorious advocates of Marxism- Stalin and Mao Zedong were the most brutal genocidal maniacs the world has ever known, responsible for the murder of countless millions of people.

But they were surely misunderstood- and more importantly, we can learn from their mistakes as we move forwards with the new friendlier, non-murdery Marxism for the twenty first century!

Let us always remember the words once spoken by that multi-millionaire, multiple property owning Über-Marxist, John Lennon- 'Imagine no possessions, I wonder if you can...Imagine all the people, sharing all the world.'. He's gone of course, but his authentic words of integrity will echo through the ages.

Meat:

Animals that have been murdered, gutted, sliced-up, burned with fire and plopped in front of you at the dinner table.

And now you're going to eat them.

Tosser.

I hope every animal you've ever eaten, rises from the dead in unison, finds you, sits on you, crushes you into mince, then force feeds you to your children as burgers.

Minority:

Congratulations!- If you are a member of any kind of subculture within society, then you qualify automatically for victimhood status. This is great news for you!

Without doubt, it's tough not fitting in with the crowd.

Nobody could deny that you have been terribly vulnerable to vile discrimination at the hands of those who represent the majority- namely straight, white men.

Don't be ashamed to acknowledge it, you have been horribly victimised.

And don't hesitate to cash-in on your victimhood status.

All you need to do is think of an individual you've met, or some organisation that you've had dealings with, who you think may have subjected you to 'hate crime' or 'hate speech'.

Take them to court, watch them squirm, pocket whatever tasty settlement you manage to wangle out of them, then skip off into the sunset with your well-earned loot.

Let us never forget, that this country, nay the whole world, is skewed entirely in favour of straight, white men.

If you are black, or brown, or female, or gay, or a midget, or autistic, or a paedophile then your life is made a constant misery in the UK- purely because you don't fit in.

To the straight, white folk you're a freak, a joke, an abomination, a god-error.

If they could get away with it, they'd like to put you all on a tanker, sail you out to the middle of the ocean and toss you into shark infested waters. Or just put you all in a zoo to stare at, point at and laugh at on bank holidays.

Are you a minority?- Then straight, white men hate you.

Never forget that.

Even if you can't see the hatred, trust me it's there.

Straight, white men will discriminate against you at every turn, if you let them get away with it.

It may be so subtle as to be indiscernible, but believe me it's happening.

If you doubt for one second that straight, white men are responsible for all the evil in this world and that they hate you and want to destroy you, then simply open a copy of The Guardian, and read the truth therein, and have your faith restored.

One people, one love, one world without straight, white men- this is the utopia we must strive for.

Misogyny:

It is clear that anything negative a man might say about any particular woman in his life is absolutely never, ever based on reasonable cause for complaint, but by an instinctual and irrational, deep-seated hatred of all women.

For what possible cause could any man have to complain about the women in his life?

All women are absolutely flawless in everything that they say and do.

There is not a single woman walking the face of the earth whose actions are motivated by anything other than good intentions, and love and concern for all humanity.

Every single woman who has ever lived, acts only and always selflessly, with nothing other than kindness in her heart.

There has never been a single woman who has ever had a bad word to say about anybody- and consequently all women should be immune from any sort of criticism, especially when you consider that all women are the tragic victims of centuries of patriarchal oppression.

It's time that we all stopped judging women, even the ones who are complete arseholes.

N

Nazi:

This is a useful catch-all word for anyone who disagrees with anything we say. Chuck it accusatorily into any argument at random, at the point where you think you may have lost, it should help distract people's attention while you try to figure out just exactly what the bloody hell you're waffling on about.

 Yes, yes, the original Nazis were responsible for the murder of over six million Jews- but that's more or less the same as someone suggesting that, for instance, Capitalism isn't evil, or that women and ethnic minorities are anything other than hideously oppressed in our country, or that global warming isn't going to turn the planet into a fireball by two thousand and thirty.

If a person even considers the possibility of any of those things being true of course, it is indisputable that they are no better than a Nazi, because all Nazis were just regular people before they started engaging in exactly that sort of wrong-think.

Next time you find yourself in some kind of argument, any argument, it doesn't matter what it's about, throw the phrase 'You're just like the Nazis' into the mix. Instantly your opponent will shrink with shame, and you will have won the argument, and rightly so, because, as a Leftist, you are automatically correct about everything.

Non-binary

A person who's gender and sexuality cannot be easily defined.
In other words, someone who doesn't know who the fuck they are, who the fuck they want to be, who the fuck they want to fuck and how the fuck they want to fuck them.
Essentially, calling someone 'non-binary' is just a euphemistic way of saying they're a ditherer.
Nonetheless, it's important to respect them and their inability to make a decision. They can't make their mind up about anything, and there is absolutely nothing wrong with that. They spend their days in a permanently puzzled state of inertia, and all power to them,

it's as valid a way to live one's life as any other.

No platforming:

It has come as a massive shock to many of us over recent years, to discover that there are genuinely people out there who don't have the same views as us. It is baffling how anyone could possibly think any differently to us, as we are so clearly spot-on about everything, because we are incredibly deep thinkers.

It is important that people who don't share our views (because of their ignorance) aren't given any platform to speak on, which could enable them to spread their poisonous lies.

It is especially important that we don't engage in debate with these wrong-headed- and dare I say evil individuals, in case they use rhetorical tricks or some other dark art to make us look like we're the idiots.

The worst possible thing would be to have our belief system challenged in a public arena and shown categorically to be built on a foundation of logical fallacies.

O
Offence:

It has now been agreed by everybody, everywhere that an individual's right not to be offended takes precedence over another individual's right to freedom of speech.

It is very important as we progress towards a Marxist utopia, that we suppress ideas as much as possible, so that no-one can put forward a compelling, reasoned, legitimate argument against us without being demonised as a bigot of some description.

Only when people are not allowed to say what they believe, will we ever be able to achieve our true, noble potential as human beings.

Oppression:

It is everywhere. You can't see it, you can't hear it, you can't touch it, so some people will tell you it doesn't exist.
There are certain groups of people who enjoy far less freedom and fewer rights than others. That is irrefutable.
If you think it's not the case, then why don't you go ahead and try explaining your logic to a black guy who's just been shot by the police, just because he ran towards them waving a gun and shouting-
 'Imma kill you! Imma kill you!'
Oh that's right, you can't explain it to a black guy who's just been shot by the police, because he's dead.

This sort of injustice is happening every hour, of every day, in every street, in every town in the UK- black people being shot by British police.
How many black people have you seen shot by the police so far today? None? Good. Black lives matter.

P

Patriarchy

White men. Evil white men. Ruining the planet for centuries now with their despicable monopoly of power.
Bastard white men. Warmongering, money-grubbing, child-molesting white men.
Destroy them all.
Eradicate them.
It is the only route to true peace on this earth.
Exterminate them and let all the beautiful meek and lovely, innocent,

victimised minorities live together in splendid harmony.

Patriotism:

What sort of idiot loves 'their' country? What sort of weak character would claim their nationality as being part of their identity?

Doesn't everybody know at this point that we are all citizens of the world? THERE ARE NO COUNTRIES. COUNTRIES ARE JUST AN EVIL HUMAN CONTRUCT. A VILE MANIFESTIFESTATION OF OUR UNEVOLVED, BESTIAL, TERRIATORIAL INSTINCTS.

Best if none of us feels a sense of affection and loyalty and connectedness to the place where we live at all. That's a sure fire way to making a place a wonderful environment to live in- if no-one who lives there gives a shit about it.

Petition:

One of the best ways of filling your empty life and annoying people, is to start a petition against something that's happening that you don't like.

The internet is great (except for all the porn) because it enables you to start an e-petition, and then hundreds of other worthy bastions of social justice can sign that petition, to get some trifling thing banned, or to scupper someone's ambitions.

You don't even need any legitimate grievance to start a petition, you can start one just to be a massive pain in the arse. The world is full of people who love being a pain in the arse- and they'll all sign your petition, and eventually everything will be banned, even petitions, and we'll all be left crying in the dark, cold and hungry and alone until death comes- but at least we will have smashed the system!

Prejudice:

If we are to create a fair and free world of justice and equality, we must first educate the masses as to the importance of not judging each other on surface values.

A happy society is one where people have the intelligence and empathy to look at each other and see the whole person, and not just make assumptions about them based on skin colour, gender, class, physical appearance, shit clothes and so on.

For example, If someone is standing in front of you in an alleyway with a massive knife and a balaclava demanding your purse, your phone and

your jewellery, don't just assume from their appearance that they're a mugger- there's every chance that they could be a street performer, an artist engaged in some pop-up theatre, possibly on the theme of class struggle.
So don't run away, play along.
Hand over your valuables and let the alleged 'masked assailant' run off into the night.
There's every chance he could be back ten seconds later to reward you for your artistic contribution to the roleplay, your input in creating improvised social satire, whilst all around you the white, Liberal, middle-class audience steps from the shadows and applauds wildly at the performance piece you've been lucky enough to be a part of.

Or maybe the guy is genuinely a mugger.

Either way, the important thing is just to hand over your valuables, because you don't need them, you don't deserve them, you've not earned them, you just feel entitled to them.

Remember the crimes of your mercenary, colonising ancestors and feel deeply ashamed.

Think of all the people in the world who have nothing, while you've got a Samsung galaxy smartphone, you smug shit.

Give the mugger all of your possessions so that they can be enjoyed by someone more deserving than you, and then invite the mugger to slash you open with his big knife of justice and equality, so that it might help alleviate some of the white guilt you feel because of the despicable overseas crimes your ancestors almost certainly committed in the racist past, and the subsequent oppression that has been allowed to pass unrelentingly from generation to generation.

Privilege:

All white people enjoy a position of privilege in society.

Everything is easier for them- getting a decent education, getting a great job, earning lots of money, buying a nice house, finding a wonderful partner, having kids, staying in shape, eating healthy, rhythmic gymnastics, quadratic equations, safe-cracking. All of these things are much, much easier for white people, due to deep-seated prejudices within society, which are the despicable legacy of the hideous white crimes of our colonial past.

Only when white people's lives are a load of shit, will the scars of colonialism begin to fade.

Progressive:

Given that we are more intelligent and more empathetic than everyone else, naturally we have superb ideas on how to instigate positive change in society. All the changes we will make once the general populace finally realises we're right about everything and gives us a democratic mandate to govern the country, will inevitably make life vastly better for all people, pretty much straight away.

Everything we say and do is clearly geared towards changing the world for the better, and so naturally people call us 'progressives'. And that is what we call ourselves as well, even though it sounds arrogant and conceited, that is simply, indisputably what we are- progressive.

If only people would listen to us, and do what we say, we would transform the world into a utopia of equality and justice.

R

Racism:

It is everywhere. And we must be extremely vigilant in rooting it out. Racism, as we all know, is any white person making any comment at all about non-white people.

It has been proven beyond all doubt that white people are not entitled to an opinion about race, and any white person who expresses any views about race, whether positive or negative in tone, is a racist.

Of course, all speech is open to interpretation and it is impossible to prove objectively that someone has said something racist.
Yet somehow you can still prosecute someone for saying something racist and easily win the case, despite not being able to meet the burden of proof. Clearly, this is the justice system working at its best to help tackle prejudice in society. Thank God we live in the kind of advanced, progressive country where free speech is not fully enshrined in law.

The punishment for racism, I think we can all agree, does not go far enough, mostly as a public order offence amounting to little more than trifling fines.

It is therefore up to us as responsible, caring citizens, to take justice into our own hands and embrace vigilantism.

The internet is a wonderful resource where we can track down racists on social media and publicly shame, smear and discredit them personally and professionally over a prolonged period, so that eventually they end up homeless and starving in a gutter, their whole racist life in ruins.
Only then might they come some way to understanding what it's like to wake up every day to racism, to step outside your front door and experience racism everywhere, from everyone, all the time.

Reactionary:

Cretinous loudmouths who are opposed to progress and improvement (i.e. don't want to embrace Marxism).

Nob ends, who want to bleat on about how things were better before equality and diversity legislation came to undermine meritocracy in every walk of life and make a mockery of all our individual achievements, abilities and hard work.

OF COURSE THINGS WEREN'T BETTER BEFORE EQUALITY AND DIVERSITY QUOTAS!

Those of us who were unlucky enough to be alive back when people were judged on their own merits will all

testify as to how bloody awful it was- when women and ethnic minorities were refused jobs just because they lacked the necessary skills or qualifications.
Thank god we've put those sexist, racist days of bigotry behind us for good.

It is probable that all of these sad, reactionary fools were dropped on their heads as a child, possibly more than once. There are a great many of these people in the world, which suggests that child dropping is a common and popular activity amongst parents everywhere.
We must continue to claim the intellectual high-ground over these vermin, even if they are more

thoughtful, articulate and independent-minded than us.

We must shut them down if they try to foist their dangerous ideas on people, their irresponsible notions that things are not so bad, and that extreme social engineering is not necessary to save the human race from oblivion.

Progress depends on stifling debate, killing free speech and just getting on with the job of smashing the capitalist system and creating a glorious world where we all pretend we are equal, where there is no merit, no competition, no ambition, no excellence, no striving for perfection, nothing good and no reason to be alive. For then will we have achieved the sort of earthly paradise that people are just too ignorant right now to realise they really want.

Referendum:

There must never, ever be one of these ever again.

The great, unwashed, bigoted public are a vile enemy unto themselves.

It is an entirely illegitimate form of governance, and if there were any justice in this world, all referendums that have ever taken place would be rendered null and void.

They are truly a rank and despicable perversion of democracy.

Refugee

Angels from across the ocean. Peace loving paragons of virtue. Only wanting to escape the brutal conflict that has ravaged their beloved homeland, to take their families out of harm's way and carve out a humble life of hard work in whatever place has the kindness of heart to take them in. Ideally it would be a country with a capitalist democracy, a thriving economy and an extensive benefits system wide open to abuse, where they could live six to a room, taking on casual work for less than minimum wage, sending it home to their country of origin where mansions cost the equivalent of fifty quid.

Let it never be suggested that the line between 'refugee' and 'economic migrant' is a blurred one.

Never forget- so many of these poor individuals entering the UK in the back of a truck are victims of fortune, unlucky enough to be born in places where they have been subject to the tyranny of corrupt despots.

Let us welcome them into our homes with open arms. There's room for us all on this small island.

Religion:

A load of superstitious nonsense that should be done away with entirely and made illegal. There is no God, that's a definite fact, and so when we die there is nothing, just an eternity of nothingness.

There's no point believing in a magic man in the sky, because he's not real, nor has he ever been. And I'm sorry if that's depressing for you, but your life is meaningless and you should just accept that and crack on with all the pointless stuff you do to distract yourself until death comes.

People who believe in some God or other, are idiots.

As we all know, people of differing religions have very strong, but often conflicting beliefs about the 'correct' way for us all to live- and these irreconcilable differences have created great acrimony amongst human beings of various faiths for hundreds of years and been the cause of many brutal conflicts over the course of history.

It is only by getting rid of religion that we can ultimately all learn to live harmoniously together, with no belief system whatsoever, except for Islam. Muslims get a bloody bad press what with all the terrorism that has been going on in recent years- terrorism which we must state categorically has NOTHING TO DO WITH ISLAM.

People need to leave Muslims alone and let them get on with oppressing women, or hating gays or whatever it is they want to do, in peace.
What harm are Muslims doing anyone (apart from women and gays)?
To ensure our own survival and progression towards higher consciousness, we, the human race, need to get rid of all religion, and the only exception to this is Islam, to which we should all submit, before we get blown up.

S

Safe Spaces:

Because we are such caring, compassionate individuals, with deep levels of empathy, from time to time, being in the world and interacting with humanity, we get our feelings hurt. This is utterly unacceptable.

We are delicate flowers and we must be protected from all the badness of the world, and opinions we don't agree with, and things that are happening that we don't want to acknowledge. We need to be shielded from these things so that we can grow and flourish to our full potential.

It is imperative that there are places in this world where we can be sure that nothing is going to encroach upon our well-being and disturb our tender state of mind by challenging our world view. Universities for instance, which contrary to popular belief, are not centres of learning, but safe havens where we can make the difficult transition from adolescence into adulthood. In such an environment, it is very important that everything that even hints at being a contradiction of our Liberal values must be banned.
Speakers must be banned. Certain books must be banned. Certain films and TV shows. Certain inappropriate

ways of dressing. Certain music. Certain food and beverages. Certain words and phrases. Certain tones of voice. Certain ways of breathing must all be banned outright. Banned, banned, banned. And there can be no room for manoeuvre on this.

It is imperative that our wellbeing be preserved by keeping our preconceptions and narrow view of the world in place and by denying ourselves any sensory access to anything outside the limited parameters of our mental comfort zone.

Ideally we would all spend every day of our lives wrapped in cotton wool, in temperature controlled padded cells on a vegetable diet, doing gentle yoga and listening to the sound of pan pipes, but that is just not realistic.

We must live in the world and embrace all it has to offer, be prepared to see, hear, touch, taste, smell, feel whatever comes our way- but only once we have banned all the bad stuff.

Sexism

We can all agree that women's lives are much tougher than men's, because of the prejudice women automatically face every single day, victims of culturally ingrained oppression, second class citizens in a patriarchal world.

Yes, yes, four out of every five people across the planet who commit suicide are men, we're all well aware of that- it's a fact that misogynists like to trot out time and again in a pathetic attempt to undermine the important drive for women's equality.

The truth is, that men have everything handed to them on a plate in this despicable, patriarchal world- even the weak imbeciles that top themselves.

Feminism is the answer to creating a fairer, better society for us all. And that means hating men. The only way to smash the patriarchy is to channel your deep-seated hatred of men. Cultivate the art of lying about men, smear and discredit them and damage their reputation to a degree that eventually they'll be left bankrupt and homeless. Some of the words you can use to ruin men are- misogynist, chauvinist, predatory, disrespectful, inappropriate, intimidating, rapey, leering, gropey, suggestive, lecherous- general slurs that can't be proven, but are to be accepted without question by society. This will make men look bad, without you having the burden of having to come up with something tangible that they've actually said or done.

Remember- never be afraid to chuck a few rape accusations about. By law you will receive the protection of anonymity, whereas the individual you've accused will have their name mercilessly dragged through the gutter, and what could be fairer than that.

Snowflake:

A grossly offensive word that bigots use to describe special, empathetic people like us.

A word that seeks to poke fun at the fact that we are sensitive, caring people who just want to look after the planet. A word that seeks to ridicule us because we just want all humans to be nice to each other, and for nobody to suffer further vile prejudice at the hands of the monstrous, white patriarchy, whose hearts are filled with hate.

Yes, we get terribly upset when people use words we don't like and say things we don't agree with- and yes we do try as far as possible to destroy those individuals lives by having them banned, or getting them sacked or just subjecting them to a concerted campaign of personal abuse, be it on social media, in national newspapers, on television or in their front garden. Why should we let these scum get away with having views we don't agree with? They've hurt our feelings, they've shaken our delicate sensibilities, it's only fair that in response we react with concerted moral hysteria in an effort to ruin their entire lives.

T

The Guardian:

Page after page of truth. The only news source that really tells it as it is.
All the other newspapers print a load of lies, because they're manipulated by shady corporate enterprises that have a pernicious, evil agenda that goes against everything we Leftists stand for in our attempts to create a better world, whereas The Guardian is indisputably a shining beacon of neutrality.
Yes, The Guardian is struggling very badly for money, because people

wrong-headedly choose to get their news from elsewhere.

Yes, as a commercial entity, it is failing desperately.

Yes, it's not quite the respected publication it once perhaps was.

Yes, The Guardian has, of late, been reduced to desperately soliciting donations from anyone who happens upon their website.

But none of that detracts from the fact that The Guardian features, on a daily basis, journalism of the very highest standard, and the fact that nobody wants to read that journalism, does not lessen its vast superiority and supreme worthiness.

We'll all miss it once it's gone. Then we'll get over it and move on with our lives.

Transphobia:

If some men feel like they want to get their knackers chopped off, plastic funbags surgically inserted into their chest, laser hair removal treatment, and have their hormones medically adjusted, so that they can swank around in a dress pretending they're a women, then they should be respected, accepted and embraced (but not too vigorously, in case one of their fake tits accidentally pops.)

There is absolutely nothing wrong with pretending to be the opposite of what you are.

Yes, perhaps it's an abomination of nature, but so what? What has nature ever done for us? Nature isn't always right. There's nothing compelling us to live by natural laws.

If a thirteen year old boy says 'I feel like a woman', we should be celebrating that, and sending him off to school wearing a skirt. And when he reaches the age of sixteen, we should pack him off for extensive surgical procedures to turn him into a crude parody of womanhood.

This is absolutely the right thing to do. And it enables the medical establishment to make lots of extra sweet cash for themselves.

What we shouldn't be doing when a thirteen year old boy says 'I feel like a woman', is getting a doctor to prescribe medication to regulate his hormonal impulses, so that he feels a bit more like

what he is, which is masculine, until he reaches a suitable adult age where he can make a clear, independent decision about who he is and what he wants to be. That way madness lies.
If we start doing that to young men, we are laying the foundations of a lifetime of misery for them , which will of course impact on wider society in all sorts of ways we can't even begin to contemplate.

And equally, if a thirteen-year-old girl says, I feel like a man, we should celebrate that, buy her a fake beard, steel-cap boots, a pipe and some Y-fronts, and when she's sixteen, pack her off to get her honkers removed, and her genitals turned into a weird fake penis by qualified surgeons who are inherently trustworthy and morally pristine in taking on such noble, socially-conscious work.

Basically, it's difficult to know what anyone's got inside their trousers these days. Nobody seems to know whether they're Arthur or Martha, and that, put simply, is progress of the highest order.

Tree hugging:

A vital ecological activity that is spiritually rewarding both for the human being and for the tree- which has a soul and an internal life all of its own.

Some people will tell you that trees don't feel pain, but that has been scientifically proven time and again to be inaccurate.

Respect trees, and they will respect you (albeit silently and in imperceptible ways).

Just remember- the path of compassion, social justice and Marxist integrity can be a lonely one at times. Occasionally you may find people you see on a daily basis will start to shudder at the very sight of you- but that only means you are slowly managing to recalibrate their mindset, as part of the commendable process of coaxing them into the Leftist fold.

Having and upholding the correct political views is not always conducive to being popular, and it is at those times that you will find a simple tree can be your very best friend, and provide you with all the emotional nourishment you need.

Go ahead and put your arms around a tree, any tree, after all- they can't get away.

Trigger Warning:

We are all of us delicate flowers. Like delicate flowers we are fragrant, and beautiful, and vital and each of us makes the world truly a better place. But just like delicate flowers, we cannot flourish in hostile conditions.

We need to know that we can journey through life safely, without the risk of being exposed to anything that might hurt our feelings.

Imagine if we had our feelings hurt- that would be horrendous, the world would probably end.

It is therefore imperative that all films, books, comedy, art that might risk upsetting anybody whatsoever is either

banned, or presaged with a clear warning as to its nature.
If people are warned that the thing they are about to experience might expose them to some ideas that they don't agree with, or some realities that conflict with their world view, they can then run away from that thing screaming, and never have that experience, and continue to exist in the sacred bubble of self-absorption which is the true key to all happiness.
Let everything even vaguely contentious be banned- and if it can't be banned, let it carry the stamp of outraged disapproval upon it, so that we may steer clear of it, and flourish as delicate flowers, before withering and perishing, having embraced the bare minimum of what it means to be alive-

for in that blinkeredness is the key to comfort, safety and well-being. In that blinkeredness, is the essence of Leftism.

V

Veganism:

A plant based diet has been conclusively proven by practitioners of holistic nutrition to be up to eleven times healthier than a traditional animal-murdering diet. It must be noted however, it has also been shown to have an adverse effect on one's social life.

It is sadly all too easy, when eating with other people, for out-and-proud vegans to be thought of as sanctimonious arseholes. However, do not let that stop you from spreading the truth about animal murder.

If your dining companion is enjoying a burger, make sure you whip out some graphic photos taken at an abattoir, in an effort to change that individual, to awaken their conscience, to engage them with animal rights issues, even if that means ruining their appetite. Remember, a friend who gets annoyed at you for judging their eating habits, is not a true friend at all- and having a meat-eating friend is worse than dying alone.

Victim:

If you are anything other than a straight, white male, the good news is that you are entitled to claim victimhood.

There are many perks to being a member of the victimhood club.

Your victimhood club membership entitles you to professional and financial rewards as well as advanced social status.

All you need to do to claim your free victimhood benefits is to chuck around words like 'discrimination', 'prejudice', 'racism', 'sexism', 'equality' and 'entitlement'.

These expressions will immediately put people on edge, and they are much more likely to give you a job that you're not qualified for, a pay-rise that you haven't earned, and a whole range of opportunities that you've done nothing to merit. Remember- don't be ashamed to cash-in on your victimhood.

You know in your heart that you're not remotely a victim, that life is hard for everyone regardless of gender or ethnicity, and we're all just trying to get by, and hoping to be judged on our individual merits- but it's a dog eat dog world, so if you can successfully take advantage of the extraordinary levels of wrong-headed positive discrimination that currently exist in our society, then go for it. Cash-in! Fill your boots! Line your coffers! Feather your nest! Get it while the going's good. There's only so long we'll be able to con people with this Equality/Diversity/ Victimhood flannel, so don't miss out.

W

White people:

Marauders of the world. Thieves. Wherever they have travelled upon this earth, white men have thieved. They have thieved natural resources, they have thieved culture, they have thieved ideas, they have thieved everything from brown and black people across the planet, they have plundered mercilessly and profited for centuries, living a life of wild abandon at the sorrowful expense of oppressed brown and black people. And now it is the white man's turn to be plundered. Let him suffer as he has bought suffering to others over the course of colonial history.

Let's not leave the past in the past. Let's drag it into the present and use it to create more injustice, acrimony and devastation.

Forgiveness and forgetting are disciplined pursuits of peace and harmony, but sadly impossible in this instance. There must be reparation for the crimes of the past.

Witch hunt:

A perfectly justifiable way to silence any individual expressing views we don't agree with.

Find a public figure who's said something that doesn't key in with our Marxist ethos, and then smear and discredit them. Call them an idiot- or if they've got an impeccable record of academic excellence, just question their mental health, pretend they've gone crazy- after all, if they're expressing an opinion that we don't agree with, they surely must have.

Do anything you can to undermine them. Raise the suggestion that they're some sort of sex offender if necessary. If you can find someone to make allegations of sex abuse against them, all the better.

Remember- mud sticks! Once you label someone a sexist, racist, paedophile, rapist, that's what everyone believes they are, regardless of whether it's true or not. That's the magical power of pejorative labels- so use them at every opportunity!

Join together in unison and attack individuals who say stuff you don't like. Try to destroy their whole life. Don't try to engage them in civilised political discourse, just in case they've actually got a decent point to make, which could disastrously make your own views seem foolish.

Batter them down with deeply personal ridicule and make sure you don't give them any significant forum for reply.

Only once we've eliminated all ideological insurrection (through vigorous bullying) can we move towards turning this world into a glorious monument to Marxism. And once we have done that Comrades, rest assured that all your lives will be illuminated with pure joy.

Words:

It is imperative that we keep a check on the language people are using at all times, whether spoken or written, whether on social media, at work- or even in the privacy of their own homes. If that means installing sound recording devices in people's front rooms, to make sure they're not saying any things that they shouldn't be, then so be it, for the good of the state, let it be so. There are some words that must never be spoken, some thoughts that must never be expressed. There is no greater threat to humanity's continued survival than a free flow of ideas. Only the correct ideas must be put forward and the wrong sort of ideas must be supressed at all costs.

One minute you let people start saying all the wrong kind of words, the next thing you know you've got a resurgence of Nazism on your hands, and then people start whacking the nuclear button willy-nilly all over the place, and then what are we left with?- A bunch of racists in underground bunkers, chuckling with smug satisfaction at the devastation they've created, as the world slowly burns.

Working classes:

The innocent, the blameless, the downtrodden. They graft away in dignified silence. They dig your roads for you. They empty your bins. They clean your toilets. You give them a pittance in return. They do not complain. All they want is to survive, feed their families, keep a roof over their heads. They do not ask for much. They do not expect happiness. They are the unassuming and the unrewarded, the humble and the put-upon.
And when they can't work, when they can't feed their families, when they

can't keep a roof over their heads, for whatever reason, be it illness or ill-fortune- do we put our hands in our pockets to look after them?

Well yes, we're all paying a load of tax all the time constantly to help support them. And yet, it's not enough. Poverty and need still blight our society. We must all be doing more.

Take a homeless person into your house. Give them shelter and clean clothes, a hot meal. Tend for the disabled. Wipe the dribble from their face/bottom. Get out there into the world and see how you can help people, and help them as best you can.

Life has gifted you privileged circumstances, be grateful, be humble and give something back.

One world, one love, one people, one million charities, all of them pretty vague about where the money's going, pick one and support it, you selfish prick.

X

Xenophobia:

It is clear, that practically everyone in the UK is scared of foreigners.

That's why the travel and tourism industries in this country are struggling so badly. You just can't get anyone on a plane these days.

All these Little Englanders, that won't go abroad and experience other cultures. If only people would take some time off from work once in a while, take their kids off to other countries to explore other cultures and languages, eat exotic foods, bask in the glorious weather that they don't get to experience in the UK. But they won't, the vulgarians. If there's one thing British people definitely hate, it's holidays abroad.

Undeniably, up and down the UK, people have a deeply irrational fear of foreign people and foreign places, that's clear for everyone to see, and no-one could possibly claim otherwise.

Congratulations!

That's it Comrades! You are now satisfactorily re-educated!

Get out there and put everyone on edge by being incessantly outraged at all the little things you vaguely disagree with.

Take every opportunity to be offended to a hysterical degree.

Publicly shame anyone who says anything faintly detached from the sacred progressive groupthink that binds us all together in Marxist peace and harmony.

Create a culture of fear, where the only acceptable opinions to be aired in public are your ones.

Remember, all language must be thoroughly policed, at all times, and anyone who uses language irresponsibly to say wrong things must be annihilated!

-And people who you just instinctively don't like, for reasons you can't articulate or rationalise- obliterate them as well!

Feel free to take anything that anybody has said, and twist it and distort it, and misinterpret it, until it seems like they've said something absolutely horrendous. It's easy if you try!

Only once we've created a culture where everyone is shit-scared of saying the wrong thing, only then can we call ourselves free.

Go forth, spread the good news, let us all worship at the altar of PC tossery, in the name of the Liberal, the Feminist and the Ethnic Minority, forever and ever, Amen.

Dedicated in loving memory of the UK stand-up comedy scene, died of Liberal pretentions and moral hysteria, rest in peace. x

Printed in Poland
by Amazon Fulfillment
Poland Sp. z o.o., Wrocław